FIRST SPANISH

los animales

an introduction to commonly used Spanish words and phrases
about animal friends, with more than 425 lively photographs

CONSULTANT: JEANINE BECK

ARMADILLO

Contents

Learning Spanish

Introduce your child to Spanish from an early age by combining everyday words and phrases with lively photographs of animals big and small, on the farm, in the wild and around the home. Your child will enjoy learning Spanish. Let them look at the pictures and read and remember the Spanish words and phrases that accompany them. Say the words aloud.

 ## A NEW LANGUAGE

There is a growing need today for everyone to speak a second language. All children should have the chance early in life to have access to a new language. Research indicates that children aged 2–8 are most receptive to linguistic learning. The younger the child, the easier it is to learn. The Spanish used in Europe differs from that spoken in Latin America and the United States in pronunciation and some vocabulary. The most noticeable difference in European Spanish pronunciation is the 'th' sound as in 'cena' (theh-na) or 'zapato' (tha-pat-oh). This is pronounced in America as 's' – 'seh-na', 'sa-pat-oh'.

LEARNING TOGETHER

Children love animals, so this theme is a perfect one for introducing them to Spanish. Encourage them to look at animals, birds and other creatures and say the Spanish words aloud. They can use their new Spanish vocabulary around the home with their pets, whenever they go out for a walk and at the zoo or nature reserve. You may have some Spanish friends who can talk to your children. All this will give your children a brilliant head start when they begin formal Spanish lessons at school.

LEARNING WITH PICTURES

Children respond very well to photographs and will enjoy finding pictures of the most popular animals in this book. Help them say and learn the Spanish words for all sorts of pets, from cats and dogs to rabbits and guinea pigs. They'll discover the names of many wild animals and farm animals, too, from giraffes, leopards and elephants to ducklings, sheep and pigs. Let them use Spanish to count the animals or tell you what size or shape they are.

IT'S FUN TO LEARN

Make learning fun by using the vocabulary on an everyday basis. Children like to demonstrate what they have learnt by playing games. You could mime an animal or imitate the noise an animal makes and ask your child to say its name in Spanish. Children can build up in a fun way their knowledge of commonly used Spanish words and phrases. This will give them the confidence to speak Spanish.

uno

dos

tres

cuatro

HOW THE BOOK IS STRUCTURED

The key words on each page are highlighted and translated in vocabulary panels. Sentences on each page appear in both Spanish and English to help your child understand. At the end of every section is a question-and-answer game with a puzzle for you to do together and give the child a real sense of achievement. There is a special section on grammar, with a guide to pronunciation. The dictionary lists all the key words and explains how they should be pronounced. Reward certificates at the end of the book encourage your child to test their knowledge of Spanish and will also help develop their confidence and self-esteem.

Los animales en casa

Animals in the home are friendly.
Pets like to live with people.
Talk to playful puppies, naughty
little kittens and grown-up cats.
They'll understand you when
you speak Spanish!

Aquí están los animales

Here are the animals and birds. They have heads and eyes and legs, just like us.

¡Hola! Soy Isabel.
Hello! I am Isabel.

la niña

Y yo soy Milena.
And I am Milena.

la cola

la cabeza

Isabel

Milena

el gato

los ojos

la pata

Say it with me

| la niña | el niño | la cabeza | los ojos |
| girl | boy | head | eyes |

8

¿Qué haces, Joel?
What are you doing, Joel?

Joel

el pájaro

Vuelo como un pájaro.
I am flying like a bird.

el niño

el perro

Y yo salto.
And I am jumping.

la pata	la cola	el gato	el perro	el pájaro
paw	tail	cat	dog	bird

9

Los animales se divierten

Animals have fun. They swim and jump just like us. But we can't fly – or make honey!

¡Mira las abejas!
Look at the bees!

la antena

cinco abejas

Elaboran miel.
They make honey.

el ala

la miel

Say it with me

la antena	el ala	cinco abejas	la miel
antenna	wing	five bees	honey

10

Salto como una rana.
I'm hopping like a frog.

cuatro ranas

la pata

la mano

Sabemos nadar como peces.
We can swim like fish.

la aleta

el pez de colores

cuatro ranas
four frogs

la pata
leg

la mano
hand

el pez de colores
goldfish

la aleta
fin

11

Tengo hambre

I'm hungry. The animals are hungry. Come and help the animals choose the foods they like best.

Simón

¿Tienes hambre?
Are you hungry?

Sí, Simón, tengo hambre.
Yes, Simon, I am hungry.

el perro

la carne

Say it with me

el perro	la carne	las galletas
dog	meat	biscuits

¿Qué quieres comer?
What would you like to eat?

¿unas galletas?

¿unas zanahorias?

el conejo

¿unas cebollas?

¿queso?

¡Me gustan las zanahorias!
I like carrots!

las zanahorias	el queso	las cebollas	el conejo
carrots	cheese	onions	rabbit

¡A la mesa!

Come and eat! Some animals like to be fed. Other animals catch their own dinner when they can.

¿Quieres una manzana?
Would you like an apple?

el conejo

Manuel

la lechuga

Sí, por favor, Manuel.
Yes, please, Manuel.

la cobaya

Say it with me	la manzana	la lechuga	el conejo	la cobaya
	apple	lettuce	rabbit	guinea pig

14

¿Qué te gusta comer?
What do you like to eat?

¿leche?

el gatito

¿dos ratones?

¿tres peces?

¿un helado?

Nos gustan los peces.
We like fish.

el gatito
kitten

la leche
milk

el helado
ice cream

dos ratones
two mice

tres peces
three fish

Los gatitos juegan

Kittens play. They like chasing wool, running after balls and jumping as high as they can.

¡Mira el pequeño gatito!
Look at the little kitten!

Me gusta jugar.
I like to play.

la silla

el gatito malo

	la silla	el gatito malo	los juguetes	el gatito castaño
Say it with me	chair	naughty kitten	toys	ginger kitten

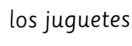

los juguetes

¡Atrapa al ratón!
Catch the mouse!

el gatito castaño

el gatito peludo

el gatito que salta

Jugamos juntos.
We are playing together.

el gatito rápido

el gatito lento

la pelota

el gatito peludo	el gatito que salta	el gatito lento	la pelota	el gatito rápido
fluffy kitten	*jumping kitten*	*slow kitten*	*ball*	*fast kitten*

Los cachorros juegan

Playing puppies have lots of energy. They love to run and play all day until it's time for bed.

Paseo a mi cachorro por el parque.
I am taking my puppy to the park.

¿Te puedo acompañar?
Can I come too?

la correa verde

las patas

el hueso
de goma

Say it with me

la correa verde
green leash

el hueso de goma
rubber bone

las patas
paws

Jugamos con cuatro pelotas.
We are playing with four balls.

uno

dos

el cachorro

tres

cuatro

Tengo una pelota azul muy grande.
I have a big blue ball.

El cachorro está cansado.
The puppy is tired.

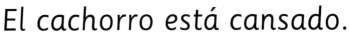

una pelota azul muy grande

el cachorro dormido

tres pelotas azules
three blue balls

el cachorro
puppy

la pelota azul muy grande
big blue ball

el cachorro dormido
sleepy puppy

¡Nos bañamos!

We're washing! Cats can spend hours washing themselves, and dogs like having their fur brushed.

Me lavo.
I am washing.

el champú

el jabón

la bañera

la esponja

la toalla

los patitos de goma

Me gustan las burbujas de jabón.
I like soap bubbles.

Say it with me

| la bañera | el jabón | la toalla | el champú |
| bath | soap | towel | shampoo |

Estamos muy limpios.
We're very clean.

dos perros

Me cepillo el pelo.
I am brushing my hair.

el cepillo para el pelo

¿Me quieres cepillar?
Will you brush me?

el patito de goma	**la esponja**	**dos perros**	**el cepillo para el pelo**
rubber duck	sponge	two dogs	hairbrush

Es hora de ir a la cama

It's bedtime and everyone is tired. Let's get ready for bed and make sure the animals are comfy.

Buenas noches a todos.

Good night, everyone.

la cesta

el gato atigrado

Estamos muy cansados.

We are very tired.

el gato rayado

Say it with me

el osito
teddy bear

la cesta
basket

el gato atigrado
tabby cat

22

Siempre tengo sueño.
I'm always sleepy.

Lulú

la tortuga

Felipe y Frida

¿Quién duerme en la cesta?
Who is sleeping in the basket?

el sueño

el perro marrón

Estoy soñando.
I am dreaming.

el gato rayado
striped cat

la tortuga
tortoise

el perro marrón
brown dog

el sueño
dream

23

Puzzle time

Here are the animals you met, but can you remember their names? Here are some clues to help you. All their names are in the word square.

El cachorro camina.

The _ _ _ _ _ _ is walking.

Los peces nadan.

The _ _ _ _ are swimming.

El conejo come.

The _ _ _ _ _ _ is eating.

Las abejas zumban.

The _ _ _ _ are buzzing.

El gatito juega.

The _ _ _ _ _ _ is playing.

El perro salta.

The _ _ _ jumps.

Find all the Spanish words in my word square

¿Dónde está el gato?

Where is the _ _ _ ?

p	e	r	r	o	v	x	c
e	w	b	h	o	c	e	a
c	a	b	e	j	a	s	c
e	l	o	f	a	r	k	h
s	e	g	a	t	i	t	o
t	k	o	e	p	r	u	r
g	a	t	o	t	n	o	r
z	s	c	o	n	e	j	o

Busca
los animales

Look for the animals. You can find them in the home, in the garden and down on the farm. Look at the pictures and then say the words aloud. You're speaking Spanish!

¿Dónde viven?

Where do they live? Each animal has a good place to live. They feel safe inside their homes.

El cachorro vive en una caseta.
The puppy lives in a kennel.

la caseta

Al cachorro le gusta su caseta.
The puppy likes his kennel.

Say it with me

la caseta del perro
kennel

la jaula
cage

el gato tricolor
tortoiseshell cat

¿Qué casa para qué animal?
Which house for which animal?

el gato tricolor

la jaula

los peces de colores

el hámster

el acuario

la cesta

los peces de colores
goldfish

el hámster
hamster

el acuario
aquarium

la cesta
basket

La casa de mis sueños

My dream home is beautiful! All these animals live in beautiful homes. Which one would you like?

¿Dónde vives?
Where do you live?

la cuerda

el barco

Vivo en un barco.
I live on a boat.

Say it with me

el barco	la cuerda	el castillo grande
boat	rope	big castle

Vivimos en una casa pequeña.
We live in a little house.

el castillo grande

la casa pequeña

la puerta

Vivo en un castillo grande.
I live in a big castle.

el piso

la ventana

Vivimos en un piso.
We live in a flat.

la casa pequeña	el piso	la puerta	la ventana
little house	flat	door	window

31

Los animales del jardín

Garden creatures come in all shapes and sizes!
Some get food from the plants in the garden.

¿Cuántas mariposas hay?

How many butterflies are there?

la planta

las mariposas

el gato

Clara

la mariposa azul

¡Hay cuatro mariposas, Clara!

There are four butterflies, Clara!

Say it with me

la planta
plant

la mariposa azul
blue butterfly

el gato
cat

el caracol
snail

¿Cuántos bichos hay en cada grupo?
How many creatures are in each group?

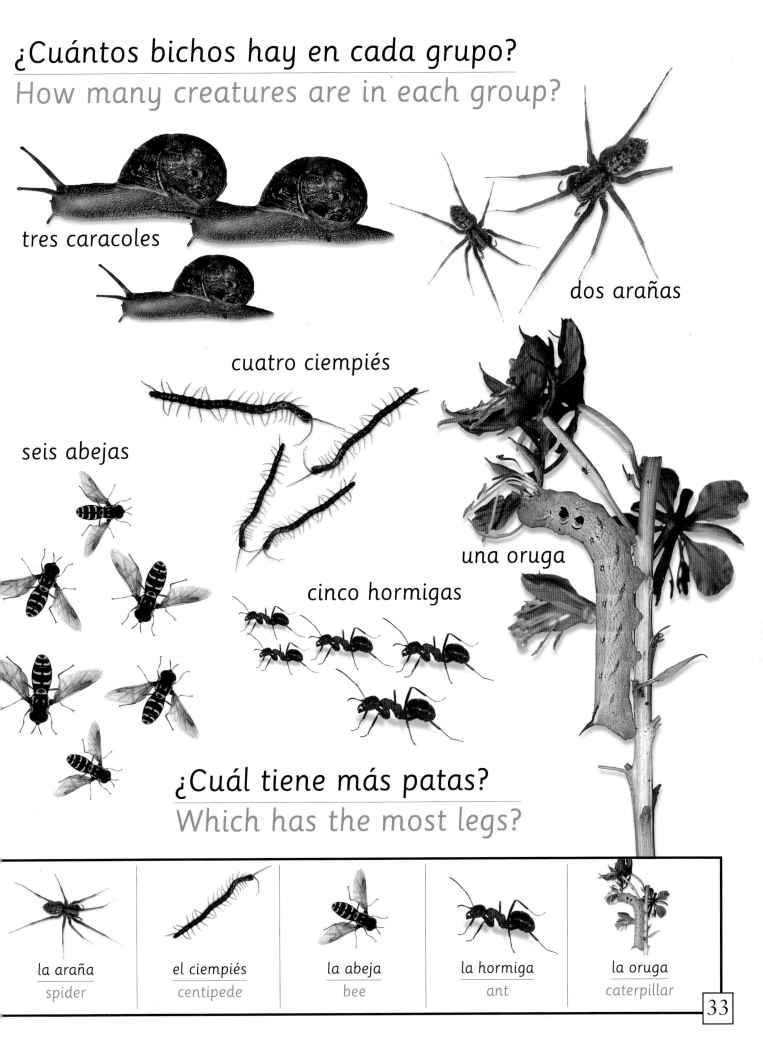

tres caracoles

dos arañas

cuatro ciempiés

seis abejas

una oruga

cinco hormigas

¿Cuál tiene más patas?
Which has the most legs?

la araña	el ciempiés	la abeja	la hormiga	la oruga
spider	centipede	bee	ant	caterpillar

Mis amigos del jardín

Garden friends can be friendly or shy. You can put out food and water for the animals and birds.

Estamos en el jardín.
We are in the garden.

las macetas

Planta la lechuga, por favor.
Please plant some lettuce.

el conejo

la cobaya

Say it with me

el conejo
rabbit

la cobaya
guinea pig

las macetas
flowerpots

la ardilla
squirrel

l'écureuil

les libellules

Il y a douze animaux.
There are twelve animals.

l'oiseau

la tortue

deux grenouilles

| l'oiseau | l'arrosoir | la tortue | les libellules | la grenouille |
| bird | watering can | tortoise | dragonflies | frog |

En la granja

On the farm, it's fun to look after the animals.
There are lots of different animals and birds.

¿Has perdido a tu madre?
Have you lost your mother?

el ternero

Sí, he perdido a mi madre.
Yes, I have lost my mother.

Say it with me

el ternero	el cerdo	la vaca
calf	pig	cow

¿Puedes ayudar a estas madres a encontrar a sus bebés?
Can you help these mothers find their babies?

los patitos

la vaca

el cerdo

los pollitos

el cerdito

el pato

la gallina

el patito	el pollito	el pato	el cerdito	la gallina
duckling	chick	duck	piglet	hen

Los animales en la granja

Farm animals need to be cared for and fed. The sheepdog helps the farmer look after the sheep.

¿Qué haces?
What are you doing?

el perro pastor

el tractor

Busco los corderos.
I am looking for the sheep.

Say it with me

el tractor
tractor

el perro pastor
sheepdog

la granja
farm

Diana da de comer a sus animales.
Diana is feeding her animals.

Diana

la granja

¿Qué comen estos animales?
What do these animals eat?

¿manzanas?

el cordero

el caballo

¿hierba?

¿heno?

la manzana	el cordero	la hierba	el caballo	el heno
apple	sheep	grass	horse	hay

Puzzle time

Animals come in all shapes and sizes, but who is the biggest and who is the smallest? Complete the Lost Letters puzzle with their names.

¿Es un hámster más grande que una vaca?

Is a _ _ _ _ _ _ _ _ bigger than a _ _ _ ?

Las hormigas son muy pequeñas.

The _ _ _ _ are very small.

¿Es Carlos más pequeño que un patito?

Is Carlos smaller than a _ _ _ _ _ _ _ _ ?

¿Es un caballo más grande que un gato?

Is a _ _ _ _ _ _ bigger than a _ _ _?

El conejo es pequeño.

The _ _ _ _ _ _ _ is small.

El cerdo está muy gordo.

The _ _ _ is very fat.

Find the lost Spanish letters

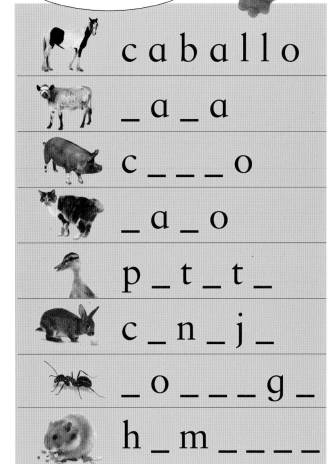

	c a b a l l o
	_ a _ a
	c _ _ _ o
	_ a _ o
	p _ t _ t _
	c _ n _ j _
	_ o _ _ _ g _
	h _ m _ _ _ _

Recorrer el mundo

Around the world are many exciting animals. You can read about them now, and one day you may see them all. Get ready by learning their Spanish names and saying the words aloud.

El bosque

The forest is a wonderful place to walk. You can find all sorts of wild animals.

Paula

Paula juega en el bosque.
Paula is playing in the forest.

las avellanas

la piña de pino

las hojas

la hiedra

¿Qué ha encontrado?
What has she found?

Say it with me

las hojas
leaves

la piña de pino
pine cone

las avellanas
hazelnuts

las hormigas
ants

¿Cuántos animales ves?
How many animals can you see?

el águila

el búho

el conejo tímido

las hormigas

el zorro

el águila	el búho	el conejo tímido	la hiedra	el zorro
eagle	owl	timid rabbit	ivy	fox

En la costa

On the seashore you can find all kinds of animals.
Look for them in rock pools and by the sea.

Isabel

¿Qué busca Isabel?
What is Isabel looking for?

las conchas

la estrella de mar

el frailecillo

la arena

Say it with me

la concha
shell

la arena
sand

la estrella de mar
starfish

el frailecillo
puffin

¿Quién nada en el agua?
Who is swimming in the water?

las gaviotas

el sol

los peces

el delfín

el cangrejo

la gaviota
seagull

el sol
sun

el pez
fish

el cangrejo
crab

el delfín
dolphin

La pradera

The grasslands are an exciting place to watch wild animals. But be careful not to get too close!

Pablo

los prismáticos

Buenos días. ¿Cómo estás?
Hello. How are you?

la jirafa

Muy bien, Pablo. ¡Gracias!
Very well, Pablo. Thank you!

Say it with me

los prismáticos
binoculars

la jirafa
giraffe

la cebra
zebra

¿Quién tiene la nariz más larga?
Who has the longest nose?

el guepardo

la cebra

el elefante

el rinoceronte

la tarántula

el guepardo	el rinoceronte	la tarántula	el elefante
cheetah	rhinoceros	tarantula	elephant

En la nieve

In the snow, you'll find lots of animals that love the cold. Remember to wrap up warm!

el gorro

la bufanda

Tengo bolas de nieve para jugar.
I have some snowballs.

¡No nos en mí!
Don't throw them at me!

el pingüino

las botas

Say it with me

el gorro hat	la bufanda scarf	la bola de nieve snowball	la bota boot

¡Cuidado!
Look out!

la foca

los niños

¡Nos escondemos en la nieve!
We are hiding in the snow!

el oso polar

la búho
de las nieves

el pingüino
penguin

la foca
seal

los niños
children

la búho de las nieves
snowy owl

el oso polar
polar bear

51

Las montañas

The mountains can be wild and dangerous.
Look out for eagles and wolves.

Antonio

¡Mira el halcón!
Look at the hawk!

el impermeable

el halcón

¡No me atrapará, Antonio!
He won't catch me, Antonio!

el leopardo

Say it with me

el impermeable
raincoat

el halcón
hawk

el leopardo
leopard

el buitre
vulture

Volamos.
We are flying.

el ala

el buitre

el águila

Puedo escalar.
I can climb.

los cuernos

¡Soy muy feroz!
I am very fierce!

la cabra

el lobo

el ala
wing

el águila
eagle

la cabra
goat

el cuerno
horn

el lobo
wolf

La jungla

The jungle is home to many brightly decorated animals. But you can't see them when they hide!

¡Soy un tigre!
I am a tiger!

¡Qué loro más bonito!
What a beautiful parrot!

la pluma

el loro

Say it with me

la pluma	el loro	el pelaje
feather	parrot	fur

¿Quién es distinto?
Who is the odd one out?

el tigre

el pelaje

la serpiente

¡Soy yo! ¡No tengo rayas!
It's me! I don't have stripes!

la rana

el camaleón

el tigre tiger	**la serpiente** snake	**la rana** frog	**el camaleón** chameleon

Puzzle time

Pablo is trying to find animals that look different. Can you help him fill in the sentences? Use the Spanish words to fill in the crossword.

1 El elefante es gris.

The elephant is _ _ _ _ _.

Pablo

2 Los insectos son rojos.

The insects are _ _ _ _.

3 El ala del loro es azul.

The parrot's wing is _ _ _ _ _.

4 El pecho del loro es amarillo.

The parrot's chest is _ _ _ _ _ _ _.

5 La tarántula es marrón.

The tarantula is _ _ _ _ _ _.

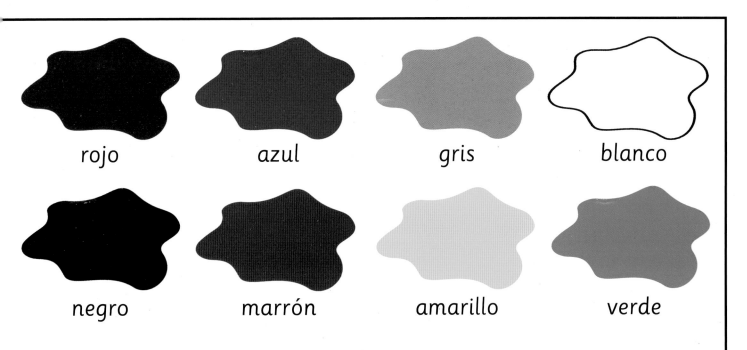

rojo   azul   gris   blanco

negro   marrón   amarillo   verde

6 La cabeza del pingüino es negra.

The penguin's head is _ _ _ _ _ _ .

7 El pecho del pingüino es blanco.

The penguin's chest is _ _ _ _ _ _ .

Now try my crossword!

8 La rana es verde.

The frog is _ _ _ _ _ _ .

How Spanish works

Encourage your child to enjoy learning Spanish and go further in the language. You may find these basic tips on how the Spanish language works helpful. Check out the dictionary, since it lists all the key words in the book and will help you pronounce the words correctly to your child.

MASCULINE/FEMININE

All nouns in Spanish are either masculine (el, un) or feminine (la, una), but this bears no relation to the actual gender of the animal (so a male tortoise is still 'la tortuga'). 'Los' or 'unos' are used in the plural for masculine nouns, 'las' or 'unas' for feminine nouns.

ADJECTIVES

As a general rule, feminine adjectives end in 'a' (e.g. la niña pequeña) and masculine adjectives in 'o' (e.g. el niño pequeño). If the adjective does not end in 'o' or 'a' it does not change.

COMPARING THINGS

When we want to compare things in English, we say they are, for example, small, smaller or smallest. This is the pattern in Spanish:

SPANISH	ENGLISH
Es pequeño	He is small
Es más pequeño	He is smaller
Es el más pequeño	He is the smallest

PERSONAL PRONOUNS

Remember that 'él' is masculine and 'ella' is feminine. The plurals are 'ellos' and 'ellas'.

SPANISH	ENGLISH
yo	I
tú	you (singular)
usted	you (singular polite)
él or ella	he or she
nosotros	we
vosotros	you (plural)
ustedes	you (plural polite)
ellos or ellas	they

'Tú' and 'vosotros' (plural) are used for talking to people you know. 'Usted' and 'ustedes' (plural) are used when you are talking to someone you don't know and are being polite.

Es un niño.

Es una niña.

pequeñas

más pequeñas

la más pequeña

VERBS

Spanish verbs change their endings depending on which personal pronoun and tense are used. This book uses only the present tense but there are other tenses in Spanish including the past and the future.

Help your child find the language pattern that emerges in the endings of the verbs. There are three groups of verbs which follow a regular pattern: those ending in 'ar', 'er' and 'ir'. Point out that in the verbs given here, 'tú' either ends in '-as' or '-es' and 'usted' either in '-a' or '-e' whilst 'vosotros' ends in '-áis', '-éis' or '-ís' and 'ustedes' in '-an' or '-en'. Play a game by saying the first word aloud – 'Yo', 'Tú'. Let your child answer with the verb – 'salto', 'saltas'.

Here are three simple verbs in the present tense. Look at the ends of the words and say the Spanish out loud.

SPANISH	ENGLISH
saltar	*to jump*
Yo salto	I jump
Tú saltas	You jump
Usted salta	You jump (polite)
Él/ella salta	He/she jumps
Nosotros saltamos	We jump
Vosotros saltáis	You jump
Ustedes saltan	You jump (plural polite)
Ellos/ellas saltan	They jump

SPANISH	ENGLISH
comer	*to eat*
Yo como	I eat
Tú comes	You eat
Usted come	You eat (polite)
Él/ella come	He/she eats
Nosotros comemos	We eat
Vosotros coméis	You eat
Ustedes comen	You eat (plural polite)
Ellos/ellas comen	They eat

SPANISH	ENGLISH
decir	*to say*
Yo digo	I say
Tú dices	You say
Usted dice	You say (polite)
Él/ella dice	He/she says
Nosotros decimos	We say
Vosotros decís	You say
Ustedes dicen	You say (pl. polite)
Ellos/ellas dicen	They say

Pronunciation Key

SPANISH	PRONOUNCE	EXAMPLE
a	*a*	*pato: pa-toh*
ai	*eye*	*frailecillo: fry-leh-thee-yo*
e	*eh*	*carne: kar-neh*
u	*oo*	*tortuga: tor-too-ga*
ui	*wee*	*buitre: bwee-treh*
b	*b*	*barco: bar-koh*
v	*b*	*gaviota: ga-bee-ota*
c	*k*	*casa: ka-sa*
c	*th*	*cepillo: theh-pee-yoh*
h	*this is not pronounced*	*hormiga: or-mee-ga*
g	*h*	*gemelos: hem-el-oz*
j	*h*	*jaula: how-la*
gu	*g*	*águila: a-gi-la*
ll	*y*	*gallina: ga-yee-na*
ñ	*ny*	*niña: nee-nya*
qu	*k*	*pequeño: pe-ke-nyo*
z	*th*	*zanahoria: thana-or-ee-a*

59

El diccionario

ENGLISH	SPANISH	SAY

A

ant	la hormiga	*la or-mee-ga*
antenna	la antena	*la an-ten-a*
apple	la manzana	*la man-than-a*
aquarium	el acuario	*el ak-war-ee-oh*

B

ball	la pelota	*la pel-oh-ta*
balls	las pelotas	*las pel-oh-taz*
basket	la cesta	*la thes-ta*
bath	la bañera	*la ban-yehr-a*
bed	la cama	*la ka-ma*
bee	la abeja	*la ab-eh-ha*
bees	las abejas	*las ab-eh-haz*
big	grande	*gran-deh*
binoculars	los prismáticos	*los priz-mat-ikoz*
bird	el pájaro	*el pa-ha-roh*
birds	los pájaros	*los pa-ha-roz*
biscuits	las galletas	*las ga-yet-az*
boat	el barco	*el bar-koh*
boot	la bota	*la boh-ta*
boy	el niño	*el nee-nyo*
boys	los niños	*los nee-nyoz*
butterfly	la mariposa	*la mar-ee-poh-sa*

Days of the week

ENGLISH	SPANISH	SAY
Monday	lunes	*loo-nez*
Tuesday	martes	*mar-tez*
Wednesday	miércoles	*mee-ehr-koh-lez*
Thursday	jueves	*hweh-bez*
Friday	viernes	*bee-ehr-nez*
Saturday	sábado	*sa-ba-doh*
Sunday	domingo	*do-ming-goh*

ENGLISH	SPANISH	SAY

C

cage	la jaula	*la how-la*
calf	el ternero	*el tehr-neh-roh*
carrots	las zanahorias	*las thana-or-ee-az*
castle	el castillo	*el kas-tee-yoh*
cat	el gato	*el ga-toh*
caterpillar	la oruga	*la or-oo-ga*
centipede	el ciempiés	*el thee-em-pee-ez*
chair	la silla	*la see-ya*
chameleon	el camaleón	*el ka-mal-eh-on*
cheese	el queso	*el keh-soh*
cheetah	el guepardo	*el gay-par-doh*
chick	el pollito	*el poh-yee-toh*
children	los niños	*los nee-nyoz*
coat	el abrigo	*el ab-ree-goh*
cow	la vaca	*la ba-ka*
crab	el cangrejo	*el kan-greh-hoh*

D

dirty	sucio	*soo-thee-oh*
dog	el perro	*el per-roh*
dolphin	el delfín	*el del-feen*
door	la puerta	*la pwehr-ta*
dragonflies	las libélulas	*las lib-el-yu-laz*
dream	el sueño	*el sweh-nyoh*
duck	el pato	*el pa-toh*
duckling	el patito	*el pa-tee-toh*

Shades

ENGLISH	SPANISH	SAY
black	negro	*neh-groh*
blue	azul	*a-thool*
brown	marrón	*mar-ron*
green	verde	*behr-deh*
grey	gris	*grees*
pink	rosa	*roh-sa*
red	rojo	*roh-hoh*
white	blanco	*blan-koh*
yellow	amarillo	*am-ar-ee-yoh*

ENGLISH	SPANISH	SAY
E		
eagle	el águila	*el a-gi-la*
ear	la oreja	*la or-eh-ha*
elephant	el elefante	*el eleh-fan-teh*
eyes	los ojos	*los oh-hoz*
F		
fast	rápido	*ra-pi-doh*
feather	la pluma	*la ploo-ma*
fin	la aleta	*la al-eh-ta*
fish	el pez	*el peth*
fishes	los peces	*los pe-thez*
flat	el piso	*el pee-soh*
flowerpot	la maceta	*la ma-theh-ta*
fluffy	peludo	*peh-loo-doh*
fox	el zorro	*el thor-roh*
frog	la rana	*la ra-na*
frogs	las ranas	*las ra-naz*
fur	el pelaje	*el pel-a-heh*
G		
ginger	castaño	*ka-sta-nyoh*
giraffe	la jirafa	*la hee-raf-a*
girl	la niña	*la nee-nya*
girls	las niñas	*las nee-nyaz*
goat	la cabra	*la ka-bra*
goldfish	los peces de colores	*los pe-thez deh ko-lor-ez*
grass	la hierba	*la yehr-ba*
guinea pig	la cobaya	*la ko-ba-ya*
H		
hairbrush	el cepillo para el pelo	*el theh-pee-yoh para el peh-loh*
hamster	el hámster	*el ham-stehr*
hand	la mano	*la ma-noh*
hat	el gorro	*el gor-roh*
hawk	el halcón	*el al-kon*
hay	el heno	*el eh-noh*
hazelnuts	las avellanas	*las abeh-yan-az*
head	la cabeza	*la ka-beh-tha*
hen	la gallina	*la ga-yee-na*
honey	la miel	*la mee-yel*
horn	el cuerno	*el kwehr-noh*
horse	el caballo	*el ka-ba-yoh*
house	la casa	*la ka-sa*

ENGLISH	SPANISH	SAY
I		
ice cream	el helado	*el eh-la-doh*
insects	los insectos	*los in-sect-toz*
ivy	la hiedra	*la yeh-dra*
K		
kennel	la caseta del perro	*la ka-seh-ta del per-roh*
kitten	el gatito	*el ga-tee-toh*
L		
leash	la correa	*la kor-reh-a*
leaves	las hojas	*las oh-haz*
leg	la pata	*la pa-ta*
leopard	el guepardo	*el gay-par-doh*
lettuce	la lechuga	*la leh-choo-ga*
little	pequeño	*pe-ke-nyo*
M		
meat	la carne	*la kar-neh*
mice	los ratones	*los ra-toh-nez*
milk	la leche	*la leh-cheh*
mouse	el ratón	*el ra-ton*

Months of the year

ENGLISH	SPANISH	SAY
January	enero	*en-ehr-oh*
February	febrero	*feb-rehr-oh*
March	marzo	*mar-thoh*
April	abril	*ab-reel*
May	mayo	*ma-yoh*
June	junio	*hoo-nee-oh*
July	julio	*hoo-lee-oh*
August	agosto	*ag-ost-oh*
September	septiembre	*sep-tee-em-breh*
October	octubre	*ok-too-breh*
November	noviembre	*nob-ee-em-breh*
December	diciembre	*dith-ee-em-breh*

ENGLISH	SPANISH	SAY

N and O

naughty	malo	*ma-loh*
onions	las cebollas	*las theh-boy-az*
owl	el búho	*el boo-oh*

P

parrot	el loro	*el lo-roh*
paw	la pata	*la pa-ta*
penguin	el pingüino	*el pin-gwee-noh*
pig	el cerdo	*el thehr-doh*
piglet	el cerdito	*el thehr-dee-toh*
pine cone	la piña de pino	*la pee-nya deh pee-noh*
plant	la planta	*la plan-ta*
polar bear	el oso polar	*el oh-soh poh-lar*
puffin	el frailecillo	*el fry-leh-thee-yoh*
puppy	el cachorro	*el ca-chor-roh*

R

rabbit	el conejo	*el kon-eh-hoh*
raincoat	el impermeable	*el im-pehr-meh-a-bleh*
rhinoceros	el rinoceronte	*el ree-noth-ehr-on-teh*
rope	la cuerda	*la kwehr-da*
rubber bone	el hueso de goma	*el weh-soh deh goh-ma*
rubber duck	el patito de goma	*el pa-tee-toh deh goh-ma*

Numbers

ENGLISH	SPANISH	SAY
1 one	uno (m.)/una (f.)	*oo-no/oo-na*
2 two	dos	*dos*
3 three	tres	*tres*
4 four	cuatro	*kwa-troh*
5 five	cinco	*thing-koh*
6 six	seis	*seh-ees*
7 seven	siete	*see-eh-teh*
8 eight	ocho	*och-oh*
9 nine	nueve	*noo-eh-beh*
10 ten	diez	*dee-eth*

S

sand	la arena	*la ar-eh-na*
scarf	la bufanda	*la boo-fan-da*
seagull	la gaviota	*la ga-bee-oh-ta*
seal	la foca	*la foh-ka*
shampoo	el champú	*el cham-poo*
sheep	el cordero	*el kor-dehr-oh*
sheepdog	el perro pastor	*el per-roh pa-stor*
shell	la concha	*la kon-cha*
sleepy	dormido	*dor-mee-doh*
slow	lento	*len-toh*
small	pequeño	*pe-ke-nyoh*
snail	el caracol	*el kara-kol*
snake	la serpiente	*la sehr-pee-enteh*
snowball	la bola de nieve	*la boh-la deh nee-eh-beh*
snowy owl	el búho de las nieves	*el boo-oh deh las nee-eh-behz*
soap	el jabón	*el ha-bon*
spider	la araña	*la ar-anya*
sponge	la esponja	*la es-pong-ha*
spotty	manchado	*man-cha-doh*
squirrel	la ardilla	*la ar-dee-ya*
starfish	la estrella de mar	*la es-treh-ya deh mar*
striped	rayado	*ra-ya-doh*
sun	el sol	*el sol*

T and V

tail	la cola	*la koh-la*
tarantula	la tarántula	*la ta-ran-too-la*
teddy bear	el osito	*el os-ee-toh*
tiger	el tigre	*el tee-greh*
timid	tímido	*teem-i-doh*
tortoise	la tortuga	*la tor-too-ga*
towel	la toalla	*la toh-a-ya*
toys	los juguetes	*los hoo-geht-ehz*
tractor	el tractor	*el trak-tor*
vulture	el buitre	*el bwee-treh*

W and Z

watering can	la regadera	*la reh-ga-dehr-a*
window	la ventana	*la ben-ta-na*
wing	el ala	*el a-la*
wolf	el lobo	*el loh-boh*
zebra	la cebra	*la theh-bra*

This is to certify that

_____

can count
from one to ten
in Spanish

Date _____

This is to certify that

_____

can say
six shades
in Spanish

Date _____

This is to certify that

_____

can say
six bird names
in Spanish

Date _____

This is to certify that

_____

can say
six animal names
in Spanish

Date _____

This edition is published by Armadillo, an imprint of Anness Publishing Ltd, 108 Great Russell Street, London WC1B 3NA; info@anness.com

www.annesspublishing.com; www.armadillobooks.co.uk; twitter: @Anness_Books

If you like the images in this book and would like to investigate using them for publishing, promotions or advertising, please visit our website www.practicalpictures.com for more information.

A CIP catalogue record for this book is available from the British Library.

Publisher: Joanna Lorenz
Editor: Joy Wotton
Editorial Consultant: Christine Younger
Design: Maggi Howells
Photography: Jane Burton, John Daniels, John Freeman,
  Robert Pickett, Kim Taylor, Lucy Tizard

The publishers would like to thank all the children who appear in this book and Martin B. Withers/FLPA – Images of Nature for the photograph on page 51 top right.

PUBLISHER'S NOTE
The author and publishers have made every effort to ensure that this book is safe for its intended use, and cannot accept any legal responsibility or liability for any harm or injury arising from misuse.

Manufacturer: Anness Publishing Ltd, 108 Great Russell Street, London WC1B 3NA, England
For Product Tracking go to: www.annesspublishing.com/tracking
Batch: 4278-23446-1127

Y ahora, ¡tú sabes hablar español!